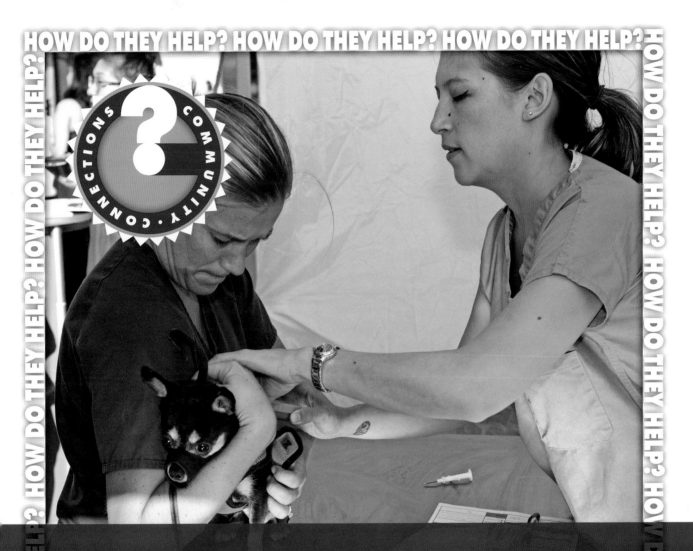

COMMUNITY CONNECTIONS **?**

HOW DO THEY HELP?
THE HUMANE SOCIETY
BY KATIE MARSICO

Published in the United States of America by Cherry Lake Publishing
Ann Arbor, Michigan
www.cherrylakepublishing.com

Content Adviser: Rob Fischer, Ph.D., Professor and Director, Master of Nonprofit
Organizations, Jack, Joseph, and Morton Mandel School of Applied Social Sciences,
Case Western Reserve University
Reading Adviser: Marla Conn MS, Ed., Literacy specialist, Read-Ability, Inc.

Photo Credits: © a katz/Shutterstock, cover, 1, 21; © Yuri Kravchenko/Shutterstock, 5;
© BMJ/Shutterstock, 7; © Mirrorpix/Newscom, 9; © Everett Collection/Shutterstock, 11;
© The Protected Art Archive / Alamy Stock Photo, 13; © Bruce Weber/Shutterstock, 15;
© s_bukley/Shutterstock, 17; © Dusan Petkovic/Shutterstock, 19

LIBRARY OF CONGRESS CATALOGING-IN-PUBLICATION DATA
Names: Marsico, Katie, 1980- author.
Title: The humane society / by Katie Marsico.
Description: Ann Arbor : Cherry Lake Publishing, 2016. | Series: How do they help? |
    Includes bibliographical references and index.
Identifiers: LCCN 2015048727| ISBN 9781634710503 (hbk) |
    ISBN 9781634712484 (pbk.) | ISBN 9781634711494 (pdf) |
    ISBN 9781634713474 (ebk)
Subjects: LCSH: Animal welfare—Societies, etc.—Juvenile literature. |
Animal rights—Juvenile   literature. | Nonprofit organizations—Juvenile literature.
Classification: LCC HV4702 .M37 2016 | DDC 179/.306—dc23
LC record available at http://lccn.loc.gov/2015048727

Cherry Lake Publishing would like to acknowledge the
work of The Partnership for 21st Century Skills. Please
visit www.p21.org for more information.

Printed in the United States of America
Corporate Graphics
CLFA11

THE HUMANE SOCIETY

CONTENTS

HOW DO THEY HELP?

COMBATING CRUELTY

Many pets live with people who love and care for them. Sadly, this is not the case for all animals. In the United States and Canada alone, millions of dogs and cats are without homes. Others experience **neglect** or **abuse**.

Humane societies help these creatures. A humane society is a **nonprofit** organization that helps protect animals.

Animals need many of the same things we do to survive.

THINK!

Think about the different roles that animals play in humans' lives. Now think about some of the challenges that animals face. Why do you think it's important for people to take steps to protect them?

5

Humane societies are found all over the world. They include the Humane Society of the United States (HSUS) and the Canadian Federation of Humane Societies (CFHS). These groups try to ensure that animals are treated with respect and **compassion**.

The HSUS and CFHS help pets. They also help animals involved in scientific research, farming, and entertainment.

Humane society workers help care for a black bear cub.

LOOK!

Find photos of HSUS and CFHS workers in action! (Hint: Try looking in magazines or online.) What are these organizations doing to improve the lives of the animals pictured?

7

A HISTORY OF HUMANE SOCIETIES

The first humane society was formed in London, England, in 1824 as the Royal Society for the Prevention of Cruelty to Animals. Its members were concerned with improving the **welfare** of the pit pony, a small horse that helped in coal mines. Pit ponies were often overworked, underfed, and abused.

The hard lives of pit ponies like this one helped to inspire the creation of the Humane Society.

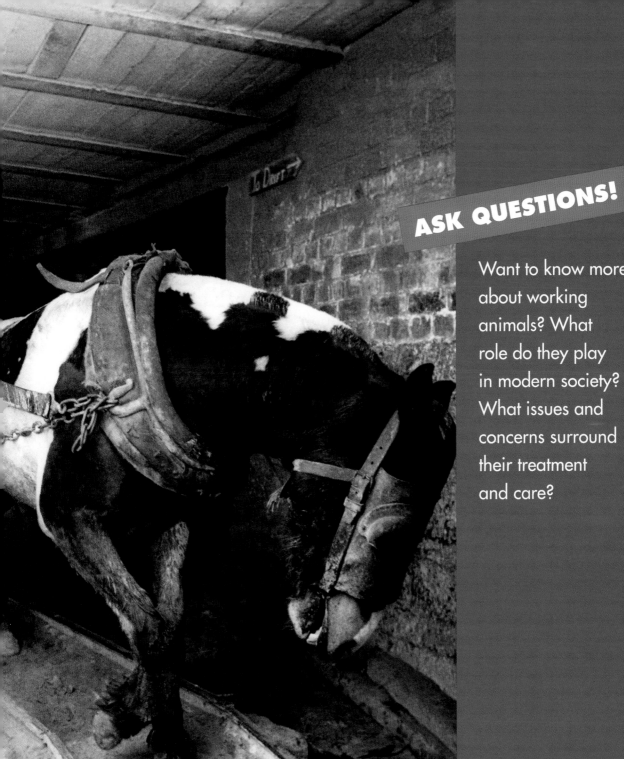

Want to know more about working animals? What role do they play in modern society? What issues and concerns surround their treatment and care?

Members of London's humane society raised public awareness about the cruelty that pit ponies experienced. They also succeeded in creating laws to protect working animals.

Eventually, people began forming humane societies outside of England. These groups focused on several different animal welfare issues. In some cases, members **lobbied** for better treatment of farm animals. In others, they built shelters for **strays** and unwanted pets.

Animals do a lot of work for humans. Humane societies make sure these animals are well cared for.

THINK!

Think about the work that animal shelters and rescues do. Many run adoption programs to help unwanted pets find new homes. Why do you think adopting an animal is often a better choice than buying one from a pet store?

11

U.S. citizens formed the HSUS in 1954. Three years later, residents of Canada founded the CFHS. These organizations helped unite smaller, local animal-welfare groups throughout the two countries that had been operating since the 1860s. They made it easier to address animal-welfare issues at a national level.

Small animal rescue organizations like this one were the foundation for the Humane Societies in the United States and Canada.

Can you guess where the HSUS and CFHS get the money they need to operate? Did you say that most of their funding comes from membership dues and donations? If you did, you'd be right!

13

Today, the HSUS and CFHS depend on several types of workers to protect animals. These include veterinarians, **biologists**, and experts in animal behavior. Lawyers and criminal investigators are other examples of humane society employees. Volunteers also donate their time and effort to help the organizations prevent animal suffering.

Many veterinarians work closely with their local Humane Society.

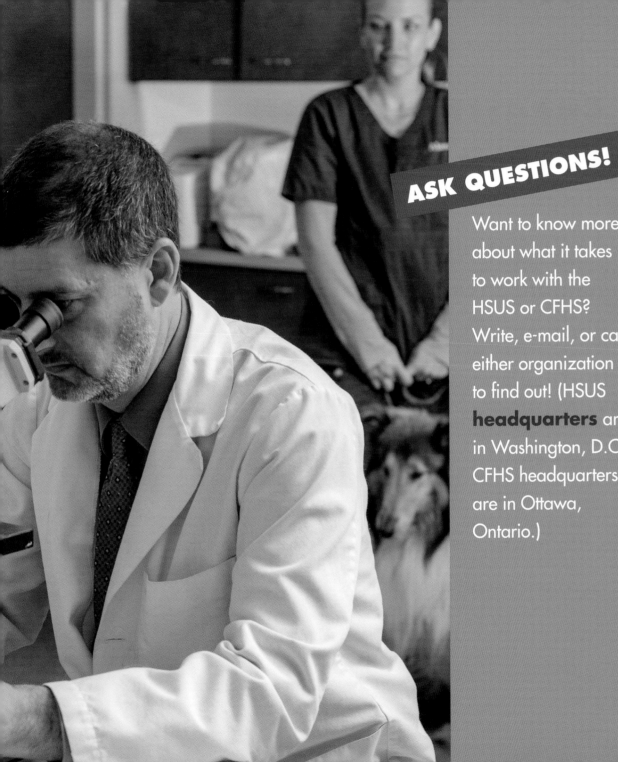

Want to know more
about what it takes
to work with the
HSUS or CFHS?
Write, e-mail, or call
either organization
to find out! (HSUS
headquarters are
in Washington, D.C.
CFHS headquarters
are in Ottawa,
Ontario.)

15

CREATING A KINDER WORLD

The HSUS and CFHS support the humane treatment of animals. They often carry out investigations. They observe how animals are being cared for in a variety of settings. These range from circuses and laboratories to farms and people's homes. They also pay close attention to threats that wild animals face, including illegal hunting.

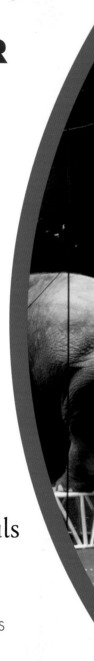

Many circuses have pledged to stop using elephants in their performances.

Can you guess how many animals are assisted by organizations such as the HSUS? Think big! The HSUS reports that it helps provide hands-on care to more than 100,000 animals each year.

If the HSUS and CFHS find that abuse or neglect is occurring, they sometimes conduct rescue operations. They help suffering animals receive medical care and shelter.

The HSUS and CFHS also work closely with government officials. They try to create laws that prevent animal cruelty from occurring in the first place.

All animals should be treated fairly—this includes animals on farms, in circuses and movies, and in your own neighborhood.

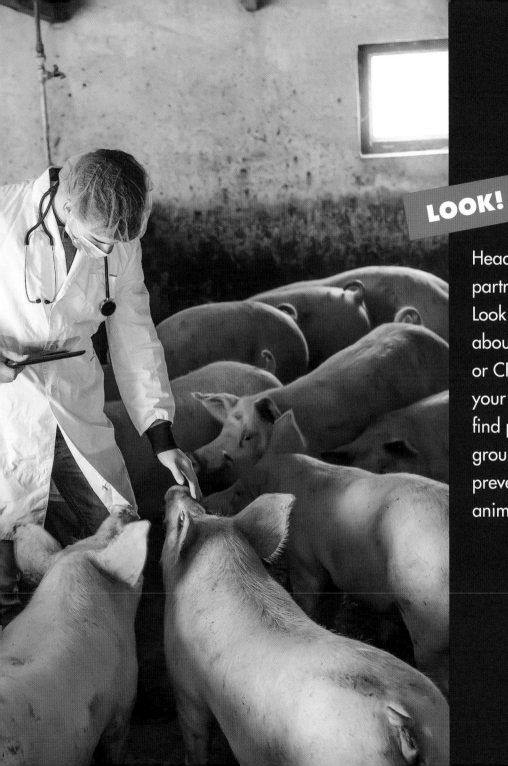

LOOK!

Head online with a partner or teacher. Look for information about what the HSUS or CFHS is doing in your area. Can you find photos of either group helping to prevent local animal cruelty?

19

Finally, a large part of what the two organizations do involves education. They offer training programs for animal-welfare groups that teach workers how to assist animals in need.

The HSUS and CFHS also organize media campaigns to raise public awareness about animal-welfare issues. This helps shape a more humane world. Since animals cannot speak for themselves, it is up to humans to protect them.

20

Caring for neglected and injured animals is an important job.

Are you interested
in supporting the
HSUS and CFHS?
Grab some crayons,
markers, and poster
board. Create posters
explaining animal-
welfare issues that
these groups are
trying to address.
Ask if you can hang
them around
your community!

21

GLOSSARY

abuse (ah-BEUSE) improper treatment

biologists (bye-AH-luh-jists) scientists who study living things, including plants and animals

compassion (kuhm-PAH-shuhn) pity and concern for the suffering of others

headquarters (HED-kwor-tuhrz) the site of an organization's main group of offices or meeting areas

humane (hyoo-MAYNE) demonstrating compassion

lobbied (LAH-beed) sought to influence lawmakers or public officials on a particular issue

neglect (nih-GLEKT) the state of being uncared for

nonprofit (nahn-PRAH-fit) not existing for the main purpose of earning more money than is spent

strays (STRAYZ) animals such as cats and dogs that are lost and have no home

welfare (WEL-fair) the happiness, health, and well-being of an individual or group

FIND OUT MORE

BOOKS

Clendening, John. *Animal Shelters*. New York: PowerKids Press, 2015.

Cohn, Jessica. *Protecting Animals*. Huntington Beach, CA: Teacher Created Materials, 2013.

Coster, Patience. *Animal Rights*. New York: Rosen Central, 2013.

WEB SITES

Canadian Federation of Humane Societies—Hey Kids!
cfhs.ca/info/kids_only_1
Head here for links to several other kid-friendly sites that discuss preventing animal cruelty.

The Humane Society of the United States—Just for Kids
www.humanesociety.org/parents_educators/kids/kids/
Visit this Web page to read articles about animal welfare and to learn more about supporting the HSUS.

INDEX

24

ABOUT THE AUTHOR

Katie Marsico is the
author of more than
200 children's books.
She lives in a suburb
of Chicago, Illinois,
with her husband
and children.